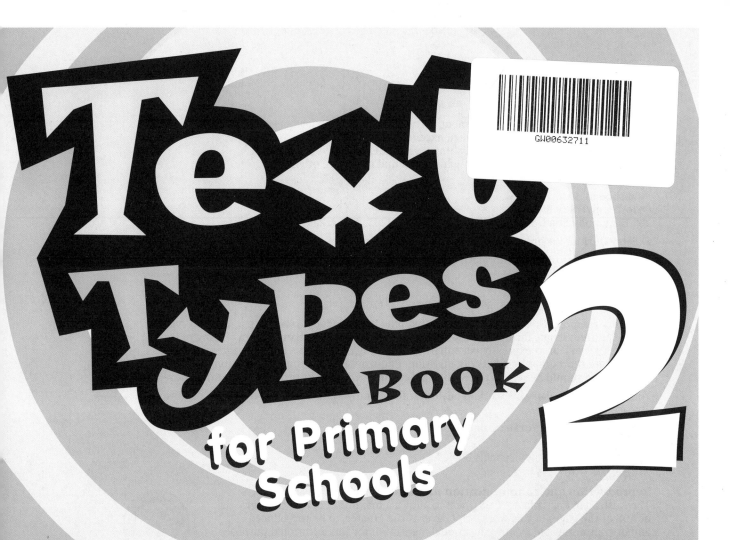

Text Types Book 2

for Primary Schools

Second Edition

Peter Durkin • Virginia Ferguson • Geoff Sperring

OXFORD
UNIVERSITY PRESS
AUSTRALIA & NEW ZEALAND

OXFORD
UNIVERSITY PRESS

Oxford University Press is a department of the University of Oxford.
It furthers the University's objective of excellence in research,
scholarship, and education by publishing worldwide. Oxford is a registered
trademark of Oxford University Press in the UK and in certain other
countries.

Published in Australia by
Oxford University Press
253 Normanby Road, South Melbourne, Victoria 3205, Australia

© Peter Durkin, Virginia Ferguson and Geoff Sperring 2006

The moral rights of the author have been asserted

First published 2001
Second edition published 2006
Reprinted 2007 (twice), 2008, 2009, 2010, 2011, 2012

National Library of Australia Cataloguing-in-Publication data

Durkin, Peter
Text Types for Primary Schools Book 2
ISBN 978 0 19 555546 2

Edited by Sally Cowan
Second edition illustrated by Luke Jurevicius
Cover illustration by Nick Diggory
Typeset by watershed art and design
Printed in Hong Kong by Sheck Wah Tong Printing Press Ltd

Contents

Introduction

Text Types for Primary Schools, Second Edition, develops students' knowledge and understanding of texts and how they are structured. This knowledge will help students to create different spoken and written texts, as well as to interpret and respond more effectively to varied texts they will encounter throughout their lives. The text types highlighted in this series are stressed in all current state curriculum documents.

The series consists of seven consumable student workbooks, a *Starter Book* and Books 1–6, which each provide 26 units of work for use in teaching specific text types. Each unit consists of a double-page spread which includes text models and space for the student to practise writing in the text type.

All books in this series cover the following text types:

Factual texts	Literary texts
recount	narrative
transaction	information narrative
report	poetry
procedure	
persuasive	
explanation	
biography	

The books have been designed to give students the opportunity to practise writing over an extended period. Thus, three or more units are generally dedicated to each text type. These are presented in developmental order, from least challenging to most challenging.

How to use this book

Before beginning the activity, extensive discussion should take place.

The following teaching techniques should be incorporated into each unit's work, in order to maximise benefits from the modelled text types:

- **Model** the text type—by showing and sharing how writing is devised.
- **Discuss and display** what the students need to learn next; for example, how to gather and sort information.
- **Show** how text types can be linked and compared; for example, by recognising similarities and differences between text types. Once students understand the fundamental characteristics of a specific text type, they are better prepared to practise writing in the specific text type.

RIGHT PAGE

Activity page

Provides space
for students to
practise the
text type.

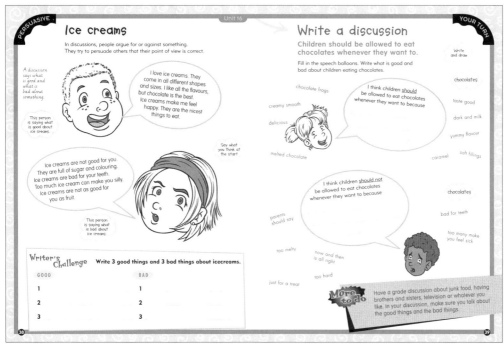

The activities throughout all books allow students to develop the following skills, which
are critical in the writing of text types:

- observation—describing what one sees
- listening—to instructions and other students' opinions
- memory—recalling what one has learnt
- questioning—asking questions of oneself and others
- thinking—working out problems
- transference—transferring knowledge from one text type to another
- cooperative skills—working within a group.

Assessment

Each book incorporates a strong assessment component, in order to allow for
self-assessment and teacher assessment of individual students:

- Student self-assessment page—allows students to assess their own understandings,
  knowledge and skills in writing specific text types.
- Student progress chart—helps the teacher keep track of the student's work,
  and is a valuable assessment tool.

Scope and sequence chart

BOOK 2

TEXT TYPE	UNITS

Recount

A recount records a series of events in the order in which they occurred. It tells how, what, where and when. Examples of recounts include:

▲ diaries

▲ letters/postcards

▲ journals

▲ autobiographies and biographies.

1 The big fish

2 The new playground

3 Dog in the fridge

4 I fell in the river

Transaction

A transactional text is used to sustain relationships and involves simple interactions and negotiations, often in the form of letters, cards and invitations.

5 A birthday card

6 A letter from Virginia

Report

A report classifies and describes general classes of phenomena. A report is accurate and factual, and uses clear, straight-forward language.

7 The shapes of leaves

8 From sheep to jumper

9 Butterflies

10 Chickens

Procedure

A procedure tells how to achieve a goal or an outcome through a sequence of steps. Examples of procedures include:

▲ instruction manuals

▲ recipe books

▲ safety manuals

▲ science books.

11 How to grow trees on tiny islands

12 How to make a floating flower

13 How to make a green hairy thing

14 How to play Scissors, Paper, Rock

TEXT TYPE	UNITS

Persuasive text

A persuasive text persuades the reader to agree with a point of view. Examples of persuasive texts include:

▲ advertisements
▲ pamphlets
▲ references
▲ posters
▲ book and film reviews.

Explanation

An explanation describes in scientific terms how natural and technological phenomena come into being.

Explanations are written to add to our store of knowledge.

Narrative

A narrative tells a realistic or imagined story. It is written to entertain, stimulate, motivate, guide and teach the reader. Examples of narratives include myths, legends, fables, fairy tales, short stories and picture books.

Structure:

▲ Orientation (setting the scene)
▲ Complication (problems/conflict)
▲ Series of events
▲ Resolution (solution of problems)

Poetry

Poetry helps us to think about familiar things in different ways. It uses language, rhythm, rhyme and structure to capture the essence of a feeling, thought, object or scene. Forms of poetry include cinquain, haiku, limericks, diamante, lyrics, ballads, humorous verse.

RECOUNT

The big fish

Structure

Title

Setting
When? Who?
Where? What?

What
happened?
(event)

Conclusion

The big fish

One day I went to a secret fishing place. I hooked a whopper. I thought it was a shark.

 The big fish tugged at my fishing rod. I had to get Grandpa to help me. After about two minutes we got the big fish onto our boat, but I was kind. I took the hook out of its mouth and put it back in the water.

 I said, "Bye-bye".

Writer's Challenge

The words in the boxes retell what happened. Draw a picture in each box. Number the boxes.

One day I went fishing.

I hooked a whopper.

We got the big fish into our boat.

I put it back in the water

Write a recount
Grandmas and grandpas

Write a recount about a special time you had with your grandma or grandpa. You could write about a holiday you had, a special day such as a visit to the beach or the circus, or about something unusual or exciting that you did with them.

Title _____

Setting   Who?   When?   Where?   What?

_____

_____

_____

_____

Events in order   What happened?

Event 1 _____

_____

Event 2 _____

_____

Event 3 _____

_____

Conclusion _____

_____

_____

More to do

Write a letter to your grandparents. Tell them about the interesting things you have been doing at school or at home. Make sure you retell all the events in the right order.

RECOUNT

The new playground

The new playground

Structure

Title

Setting
Who? Where?
When?

*What
happened?*

Conclusion

Author

Language featu

I went to the new playground with 2J today.

I wanted to go on the monkey bars. It was good fun. The monkey bars are made of metal. I went on the parallel bars and the chain bridge. Ivy jumped on the bridge.

I hope Mrs Johnson lets us play there again. "Please".

Chad

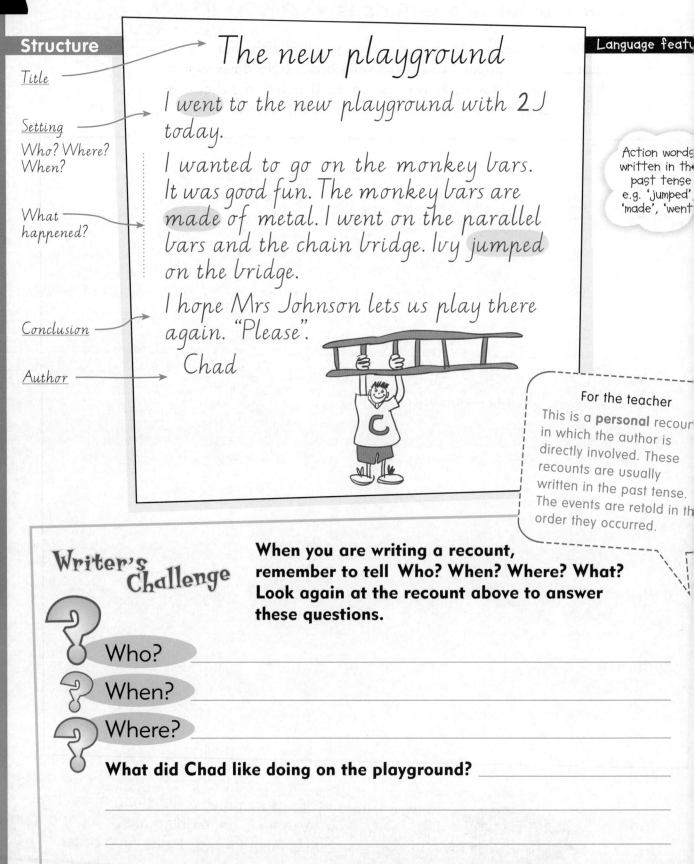

Action words
written in th
past tense
e.g. 'jumped'
'made', 'went

For the teacher

This is a **personal** recou
in which the author is
directly involved. These
recounts are usually
written in the past tense.
The events are retold in th
order they occurred.

Writer's Challenge

When you are writing a recount,
remember to tell Who? When? Where? What?
Look again at the recount above to answer
these questions.

Who? _____

When? _____

Where? _____

What did Chad like doing on the playground? _____

_____

_____

_____

Write a recount

Spotlight in the Dark—Sally's recount

Sally has written a recount about her special game.
Read it and then fill in the four W balloons.

> Spotlight in the Dark is a form of Hide-and-Seek. The searcher has a torch and when he or she shines it on the hider, that person is OUT!

Last Saturday (30th July) at about 7 pm the four of us decided to play 'Spotlight in the Dark', in our backyard.

Nathan, Chris and Yang hid while I counted to one hundred. I had the torch.

"Coming, ready or not!" I yelled.

I heard a giggle in the bushes. I shone the torch— and there was Chris. "You're out!" I shouted.

Next I found Nathan up the apple tree.

The three of us searched and searched but we couldn't find Yang.

"We give up!" we called.

The wheelie bin tumbled over and out crawled Yang!

Sally

Who was there?

Nathen and Yang chris sally

Where?

in the backyard

When?

saturday 30th july

What happened?

Played spot light in the dark

Make a wall diary. Add a new event each day.
At the end of the week, staple the pages together.

Dog in the fridge

Structure

Title

Orientation
Who? When?
Where? Why?

Events in order
What
happened?

Conclusion
How did it end?

Author

Language featu

Dog in the fridge

This happened when I was only one year old. I tried to tell Mum that Celeste had put the dog in the fridge – but it was no use. I couldn't talk!

Then my Grandpa went to get a drink. He opened the fridge and said, "Amy, there's something moving in the fridge."

Mum looked in and said, "It's the dog!" Mum got the towel and dried him.

The Amadi Family
from 'So, What's Your Story?'
Serpell P.S.

Time words
e.g. 'when', 'th

Past tense
e.g. 'happened'
'tried', 'went'
'looked', 'dried

Writer's Challenge

When you are writing a recount, remember to tell who, when, where and what.

Draw pictures that retell the 'Dog in the fridge' story in the boxes below. Use labels.

1 Celeste (3 years old) put the dog in the fridge.

2 The baby couldn't talk.

3 Grandpa gets a drink from the fridge.

4 Grandpa said, "Amy, there's something moving in the fridge."

5 Mum said, "It's the dog!"

6 Mum got the towel and dried him.

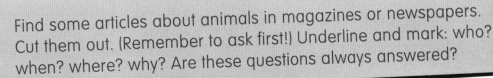

Write a recount
Animals in trouble

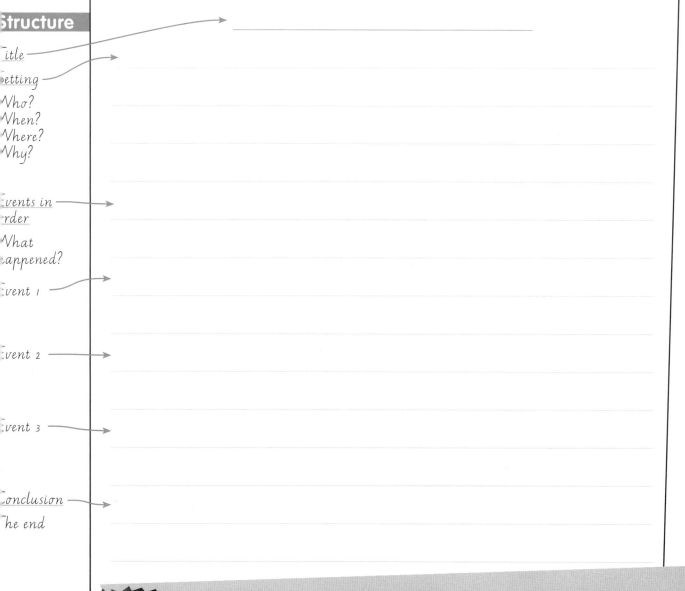

Write a recount about one of the following situations.

- An animal is lost. What animal? When did you notice it was gone? Who searched? What happened?

- A cat got stuck high in a tree. The Fire Brigade came. What happened next?

- Your puppy walked on a new wet concrete path. He left deep paw prints. What did you do?

- A dog chased a cat into a dress-up box. What a mess! What happened next?

Structure

Title

Setting
Who?
When?
Where?
Why?

Events in order
What happened?

Event 1

Event 2

Event 3

Conclusion
The end

More to do

Find some articles about animals in magazines or newspapers. Cut them out. (Remember to ask first!) Underline and mark: who? when? where? why? Are these questions always answered?

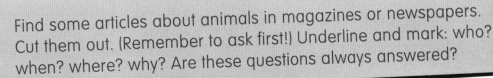

RECOUNT

I fell in the river

Structure

Language featur

Title

Setting
Who? When?
Where?

*What
happened?*

Event

Event

Conclusion

I fell in the river

When I **was** little, I was feeding the ducks and I
went too close to the water. I fell into the river.

I was **sinking**, and Mum saw a hand in the river
and she screamed "HELP!!"

A man dashed into the water with all his clothes
on and pulled me out. I was **screaming**, Mum was
screaming and the man was **shivering**.

We all went straight home and **I** was sent to bed!

Emily, Grade 2

> Past tense
> e.g. 'was',
> 'went'

> Action words
> e.g. 'sinking',
> 'shivering',
> 'screaming'

> Personal
> pronouns
> e.g. 'I',
> 'we'

Writer's Challenge

**In recounts, we tell what happened
in the order that it happened.**

> draw and
> write

Event 1 What happened first?

> draw

*Emily was feeding the ducks.
She fell in.*

Event 2 What happened next?

Event 3 What happened next?

Event 4 What happened last of all?

> draw and
> write

Write a recount
The day I saved Gina

Use the news plan below to write a recount.
Pretend that you are the person who saved Gina.

News plan— **The day I saved Gina**

When? Last Thursday

Where? Down by the river

Who with? I was fishing all by myself

Events in order
- There was a scream.
- A little girl was in the water. She was shouting for help.
- I dashed in and pulled her out. I had all my clothes on, and I was shivering.

Conclusion
- Afterwards, Gina's mum said, "Thank you so much."

Structure

Title

Setting
When?
Where?
Who with?

Events in order

Event 1

Event 2

Event 3

Conclusion
(make up your own conclusion)

More to do In your writing book, record what happened to you today. List all the times when people helped you or were friendly towards you.

A birthday card

1 The front of the card

Structure

Words in large print

Colourful pictures

3 The envelope

Braden Smith
The Snow Road
Everton Vic 3678

2 Inside message

Structure

Greeting → To Braden

Happy Birthday!

Message → Happy Birthday
Wishing you ...
chocolates
and
cupcakes
and
special cheer
on your birthday!

Your name → Love from Rima

Writer's Challenge

Make up special messages for birthday cards. They could be little poems or just special best wishes.

Make a card

Write a special message

Write a special message to a relative or friend. It could be for a birthday card, a 'thank-you' card or just a happy card.

Structure

Write the name of the person receiving the card

Write your special message

Sign your name

To _____

_____

_____

_____

_____

_____

Love from _____

The envelope

Write the name and address of the person on the envelope.

Make a real card for a relative or friend and write the above special message in it. You will need to cut a piece of card 16 cm high by 20 cm wide. Fold the card in two, so that you have a front and inside part. Draw the front of your card. Remember to write the words in big print and draw colourful pictures.

Write your message inside the card. Address an envelope, put on a stamp and post the card!

A letter from Virginia

Structure

Date

Sender's address

Address

Greeting

Information that you want to tell the reader

Farewell statements

Signature of the sender

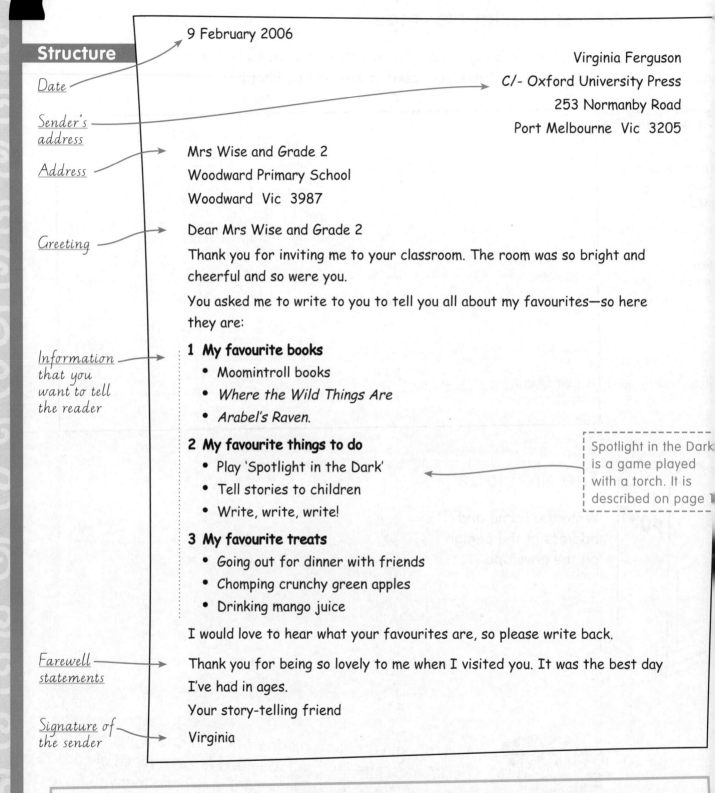

9 February 2006

Virginia Ferguson
C/- Oxford University Press
253 Normanby Road
Port Melbourne Vic 3205

Mrs Wise and Grade 2
Woodward Primary School
Woodward Vic 3987

Dear Mrs Wise and Grade 2

Thank you for inviting me to your classroom. The room was so bright and cheerful and so were you.

You asked me to write to you to tell you all about my favourites—so here they are:

1 My favourite books
- Moomintroll books
- *Where the Wild Things Are*
- *Arabel's Raven.*

2 My favourite things to do
- Play 'Spotlight in the Dark'
- Tell stories to children
- Write, write, write!

Spotlight in the Dark is a game played with a torch. It is described on page 1

3 My favourite treats
- Going out for dinner with friends
- Chomping crunchy green apples
- Drinking mango juice

I would love to hear what your favourites are, so please write back.

Thank you for being so lovely to me when I visited you. It was the best day I've had in ages.

Your story-telling friend

Virginia

Writer's Challenge

Conduct a survey. What are the class favourites? Find out and list the five most popular:

1 books   **2** games   **3** foods.

Write a letter to Virginia

Virginia is one of the authors of this book and she loves getting letters. Write to her, telling her about your favourites. Practise the letter on this page and then copy it onto another page. If she receives the letter from you, she will write back.

Structure

Date

You write it in

Sender's address

Write care of (C/-) your school

Address

Write Virginia's address from page 18

Greeting

Information that you want to tell the reader

Farewell statements

Your signature

Date _____

_____

_____

_____

_____

_____

_____

_____

Dear Virginia

I read in your letter all about your favourites. You asked me to write back telling you about my favourites—so here they are:

1 My favourite books

- _____
- _____
- _____.

2 My favourite things to do

- _____
- _____
- _____

3 My favourite treats

- _____
- _____
- _____

I would be really happy if you wrote back to me care of my school. The address is above.

Thank you and very best wishes

_____

To the teacher

Of course we cannot guarantee that the famous person will write back, but we promise that Virginia will!

More to do

Write a letter to someone famous. Think about what you want to know, then put it in your letter. You never know—you might get a reply!

REPORT

The shapes of leaves

Leaves have many different shapes

Many leaves are oval or round-shaped. Some are shaped like arrowheads or spears, and others look like feathers, hands or hearts. The leaves below come from plants that grow in different parts of Australia.

Spear shape (lance)
Sharp point looks like spear (lance), e.g. peach leaf

Oval shape
Wider than lance, pointed at tip e.g. hydrangea
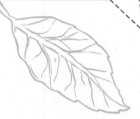

Round
e.g. nasturtium, pumpkin

Arrow shape
Like an arrow head, e.g. ivy

Needle shape
Pine tree leaves are like needles.

Writer's Challenge   **Draw the right leaves inside the shapes.**

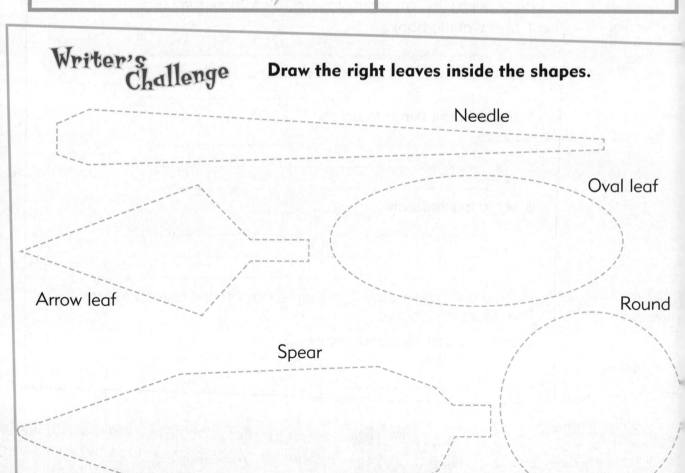

Needle

Oval leaf

Arrow leaf

Round

Spear

Write a report

The edges of leaves

Leaves have three different types of edges. Smooth-edged leaves are most common in warmer climates. Toothed-edged leaves grow in cooler places. Curved-edged leaves look as if large bites have been take out of them.

smooth

curved

toothed

Smooth edge

Toothed edge

Curved edge

Draw two leaves in each box.
Choose from the pictures below.

Write some facts about your leaf collection.

Collect leaves from outside. Group them according to their shapes. Stick the different groups onto a large sheet of paper.

REPORT

From sheep to jumper

Structure

General statement

A flow chart

The pictures below show how wool from a sheep can be turned into a woollen jumper.

Labels and diagram

1 Wool grows on sheep.

2 Shearer cuts wool.

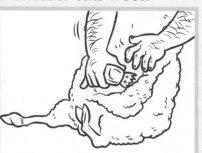

Description
Flow charts are used to describe the process

5 In factory, wool is spun into thread.

4 Wool then goes by truck or train to factory.

3 Wool is put in bales.

NATIONAL WOOL CO.

WOOL

6 Thread is woven into fabric.

7 Fabric is made into clothing.

Action verb e.g. 'spun', 'woven', 'cu

Writer's Challenge

Reports often contain action verbs such as 'spun' and 'woven'. Underline 8 action verbs in the report above.

Write a report

A flow chart
Complete the flow chart by drawing the pictures.

From tree to paper

| Trees are cut down. | Trucks take logs to paper mills. |

| The logs are ground up and mixed with water to make wood pulp. | A paper mill is a big factory that turns tree logs into huge rolls of paper. |

| A machine then presses and rolls a layer of pulp into paper. | The paper is dried and wound onto a large roll. |

What happens next?

Make a list of the things paper can be made into.

More to do Make your own flow chart on ice cream, bread, milk or chocolate. You will need to find information on your topic before you begin your flow chart.

REPORT

Butterflies

Structure

General statement

Description
Some information about the butterfly

Conclusion
A finishing off sentence

Butterflies

Butterflies are insects. The butterfly lays its eggs under a leaf so that birds do not get them. When the caterpillar hatches out of the egg, it eats and eats and eats. When the caterpillar is fat, it turns into a chrysalis for two weeks. Then it turns into a butterfly.

Dylan

Language featur...

Picture

Action verb

Technical terms

Diagra...

Writer's Challenge The life cycle of the butterfly

Show the life cycle of the butterfly by drawing pictures in the squares.

Butterfly lays eggs	Caterpillar hatches out	Caterpillar eats, eats, eats
It gets fat	It turns into a chrysalis	A new butterfly comes out

Write a report

Frogs

Use all the information in the box to write your own report about frogs.

The pictures below show the life cycle of a frog.

tail gets longer

legs

tail

body

eggs

Frogs and toads are amphibians.

Frogs live in wet places. They have smooth, slimy skin.

new frog

Structure

Title _____

General statement **Frogs are** _____

Description **Frogs live** _____

Some information about the life cycle of a frog

They have _____

_____

_____

Conclusion _____

_____

More to do

Many frogs are in danger of becoming extinct. Find out all you can about frogs and then design a 'Save the Frog' poster.

REPORT

Chickens

The fact chart helps you to sort out information.

A FACT CHART

What kind of animal is a chicken?

▲ Chickens are birds.

▲ They are a type of poultry.

• _____

• _____

• _____

How do chickens reproduce?

▲ All baby birds start life in eggs.

▲ Eggs are laid in nests and the mother sits on them.

• _____

• _____

CHICKENS

What do chickens look like?

▲ There are many types of chicken.

▲ Some are red, some are white and some are black.

• _____

• _____

What do chickens eat?

▲ They eat seeds and insects.

▲ They eat worms.

• _____

• _____

• _____

A report

The first sentence tells what you are writing about

The report uses facts from the fact chart

Chickens

Chickens are a special type of bird called poultry. They are kept by farmers for their eggs and meat. Chickens can be red, white or black, and they have red combs and wattles.

All chickens start life in eggs. They are in the eggs for 21 days and break out when they are fully formed. Some hens lay up to 300 eggs a year.

Chickens eat seeds, insects, worms and special meal fed to them by farmers.

Writer's Challenge

Read the fact chart about chickens. In the spaces in each box, add more facts about chickens. A special prize (a chocolate egg?!) for those who can write a fact in all four boxes. (You will have to keep your writing small.)

Write a report

YOUR TURN

Add some facts

Look in some books.

Use your computer.

A FACT CHART DUCKS

What kind of animal?

▲ A duck is a bird.

- _____
- _____
- _____

What do ducks look like?

▲ Ducks have flat bills.

- _____
- _____
- _____

How are ducks used?

▲ People eat duck eggs.

- _____
- _____
- _____

How do ducks reproduce?

▲ Ducks lay eggs.

- _____
- _____
- _____

Write your own report using facts from the fact chart.

Ducks

_____

_____

_____

_____

_____

_____

_____

Use your own fact chart to write a report about your pet. Read your report to the class.

How to grow trees on tiny islands

Structure

Title

Materials

Steps
The steps in order from first to last.

Evaluation

How to grow trees on tiny islands

Things you need

▲ a shallow dish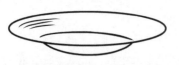

▲ water

▲ root vegetables with a few sprouts

What to do

1 Chop the tops off vegetables. Leave about 3 cm under the sprout.

2 Half fill shallow dish with cold water.

3 Place vegetable tops on bottom of dish.

4 Pour more water around the vegetable tops. (Do not cover them.)

5 Put dish in warm place, such as on a windowsill.

6 Add a little water each day. After a week or so the shoots will shoot up. They look like tall trees on tiny islands.

Writer's Challenge

When you write a procedure, remember to begin with an action word (verb). For example, 'shut', 'place', 'turn'. Find six verbs in the steps above.

1 _____   2 _____   3 _____

4 _____   5 _____   6 _____

Write a procedure

In this procedure some of the words have been left out.
You write in the missing words. Use the pictures to help.

Structure

Title

Materials needed

Steps

How to grow a prickly tree

1 ripe pineapple

2 chopping board

3 compost

4 pot

5 water

Draw

What to do

1 Place the pineapple on a chopping board. ⟶

2 Cut the top off the p _____

3 Leave it on its side for a few days until it dries out a little.

4 Fill the pot with _____

Draw

5 Put the _____ on top of the compost.
⟶

6 Pour _____ on the pineapple and leave

   in a _____ place.

Evaluation Did your tree shoot up and get even more prickly?

More to do Grow broad beans in a jar. Find out how to do it and then write a procedure.

How to make a floating flower

How to make a floating flower

Materials

You will need:

1 This shape, traced onto firm paper. →

2 Scissors.

3 Textas or pencils to colour flower.

4 Water.

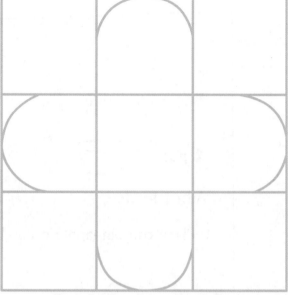

Steps

What to do:

1 Colour shape brightly before you cut it out.

2 Cut it out.

3 Fold along dotted lines. Fold each petal in towards the centre.

4 It will look like this: →

5 Place flower on water. Watch.

Evaluation

Did it work? If your flower unfolded its petals very slowly, your procedure worked. Well done!

For the teacher

• The flower will gradually unfold its petals. Children watch this absolutely transfixed in wonder. "It's magic!"

• The paper has 'capillaries' like real flower petals, and the water travels along these, thus causing the movement outwards.

Make a smaller flower, or a bigger one. Draw the shape yourself. Try to make the petals and the centre about the same size. Float them all together.

Write a procedure

YOUR TURN

For the teacher
Use same shape as flower, but keep edges straight. Make the basket with students.

Structure

Title

Materials

How to make a simple basket

1 A shape like this (it must be drawn onto firm card) →

2 Textas or pencils

3 Scissors

4 Sticky tape

You draw pictures of the materials you need.

What to do

Steps

ou draw the ictures for each step.

1 Cut out shape and colour in. The shape	**2** Fold on dotted lines. Stand edges up straight. You now have a wobbly box. The wobbly box
3 Use bits of sticky tape to hold sides together. Sticking it together	**4** Cut out a narrow strip for the handle. Stick on. The finished basket

Did your basket work? Was it too wobbly? Write on the lines below.

Evaluation

_____

_____

_____

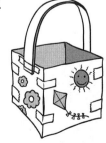

PROCEDURE

How to make a green hairy head

Structure

<u>Title</u>

<u>Materials</u>

seeds   soil   old sock

<u>Steps</u>

The steps in order from first to last

1 Put seeds in sock.

2 Put soil on top.

3 Tie up top of sock with elastic band.

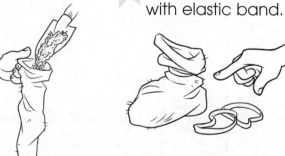

4 Turn over and put in saucer.

5 Pour on water.

6 Stick on eyes and nose.

7 Put in warm spot. Keep top wet.

<u>Evaluation</u>

If the green grassy hair begins to grow, then the procedure has worked.

Writer's Challenge

Draw a circle around all the action words (verbs) you can find in the procedure.

How many did you find?

Write a procedure

YOUR TURN

Structure

Title

Materials

How to grow a carrot tree

You do the drawings

1 A carrot top with a sprout   **2** A dish   **3** A jug of water

Steps

You write the steps telling what to do.

1

2

3

Evaluation → Did it work? How can you tell?

For the teacher
Some children may need to refer to the model on page 28 to write their procedure.

33

PROCEDURE

How to play:
Scissors, Paper, Rock

Structure

Title

Materials

Steps

Scoring

Rock and scissors:

Rock blunts scissors, so rock wins.

Paper and rock:

Paper wraps rock, so paper wins

Paper and scissors:

Scissors cut paper, so scissors win.

The same positions:

If you both make the same hand symbol, it is a draw.

Evaluation

Scissors, Paper, Rock

You will need:

Two people, nothing else

Steps

1 Players sit opposite each other. Each clenches a fist.

2 Players chant, "One, two, three". On the word "three", both players show their hands in one of these three positions.

rock: a clenched fist

scissors: two open fingers held sideways

paper: a flat hand held sideways

3 That's all. The game is over! Here's how you score: If one person shows a rock and the other person shows scissors, the rock wins because rock blunts scissors. Other scores are shown in the 'Scoring' box.

4 Start another game. Play ten games. Who won most? Play 20 or 50 or 100. Who won most?

If you liked playing this game, then it was a success. A good thing about this game is that it can be played anywhere—beach, bus, yard, home—and nothing else is needed: just hands!

Writer's Challenge

Nouns

Nouns are naming words.
Read the procedure above.
Write the nouns near the pictures.

h _ _ _

p _ _ _ _ _

r _ _ _ _

s _ _ _ _ _ _ _

My favourite game to play is

_____

_____.

Write a procedure

Structure

Title

Materials

Steps

You write the steps

Throws stone

Hops around

What next?

Evaluation

If you answered 'yes', your game was successful.

How to play hopscotch

You will need:
- A space for the hopscotch game
- A stick or piece of chalk to draw the shape
- A flat stone

What to do:

1 Draw the grid. Number the squares.

2 First person stands _____

3 _____

4 _____

5 _____

_____

Did you enjoy the game? Did other people?

Number the spaces

Starting line

> **Note**
> Most people know how to play hopscotch, but it is very hard to write down! Ask others to help.

More to do

Try a different grid.

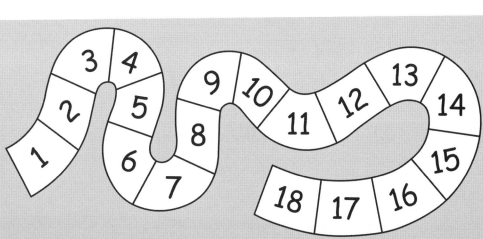

Are the rules the same?

What we need in the world

Structure

Title

Introduction

Your arguments

1

2

3

Ending

What we need in the world

Dad and I believe that we need to think more about people in this world.

I think that we need more love and peace, and less fighting in the world.

We need plants so we can breathe, and we need less pollution.

We need food and water so we can live. We should not litter the world.

Most of all we should help and think about each other.

Writer's Challenge

Say how you feel by finishing off these 'because' sentences.

For the teacher

In a persuasive text the writer tries to persuade someone to believe their point of view. An argument is provided and supporting evidence given. At Year 2 level, students will write sentences which present their point of view.

1 People should not chop down trees because

2 Wars are bad because

3 We should be kind to our pets because

4 Being friendly to our teacher is good because

Write a persuasive text
How could adults be better?

Write your own persuasive text. Use the ideas in the speech bubbles or your own.

Adults should listen to children.

Adults should play more games with children.

Adults should be kind to animals.

Adults should stop fighting.

Adults should stop being bossy.

Adults should not nag us.

Adults should stop making too many rules.

Structure

Title

Introduction

Your arguments

List ways adults could be better

Ending sentence

How adults could be better

The most important way adults could be better is

PERSUASIVE

Ice creams

In discussions, people argue for or against something.
They try to persuade others that their point of view is correct.

A discussion says what is good and what is bad about something.

This person is saying what is good about ice creams.

I love ice creams. They come in all different shapes and sizes. I like all the flavours, but chocolate is the best. Ice creams make me feel happy. They are the nicest things to eat.

Say what you think at the start

Ice creams are not good for you. They are full of sugar and colouring. Ice creams are bad for your teeth. Too much ice cream can make you silly. Ice creams are not as good for you as fruit.

This person is saying what is bad about ice creams.

Writer's Challenge
Write 3 good things and 3 bad things about icecreams.

GOOD
1 _____
2 _____
3 _____

BAD
1 _____
2 _____
3 _____

Write a discussion

Children should be allowed to eat chocolates whenever they want to.

Fill in the speech balloons. Write what is good and bad about children eating chocolates.

YOUR TURN

Write and draw

chocolates

chocolate frogs

creamy smooth

delicious

melted chocolate

I think children <u>should</u> be allowed to eat chocolates whenever they want to because

_____

_____

_____

taste good

dark and milk

yummy flavour

caramel   soft fillings

I think children <u>should not</u> be allowed to eat chocolates whenever they want to because

_____

_____

_____

chocolates

bad for teeth

too many make you feel sick

parents should say

too melty

now and then is all right

too hard

just for a treat

More to do

Have a grade discussion about junk food, having brothers and sisters, television or whatever you like. In your discussion, make sure you talk about the good things and the bad things.

PERSUASIVE

Kangashoos

Do you want to leap ahead of the pack?
Then you are bound to love kangashoos.

Kangashoos:

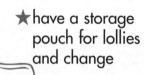

★ are made of soft, hard-wearing kangaroo leather

★ have a storage pouch for lollies and change

★ come in 6 cool colours

★ feature retractable coil springs for that bouncing on air feeling

★ have a graphite rail for extra spring

The 'must-have' shoes!
★ **Kangashoos** ★
Spring to victory!

A question at the start to attract attention

Persuasive words e.g. 'cool', 'love', 'must have'

Appealing picture

Logo or symbol

Clever langua...
that plays o...
words e.g. 'le...

List of features

Technical language 'graphite'

Saying or slogan

Writer's Challenge — Selling points

Advertising posters try to make you want to buy things.
List four things that might make you want to buy Kangashoos.

1 _____

2 _____

3 _____

4 _____

Make your own poster

Design your own sports shoe with some new and special features. Present it in the form of an advertising poster.

YOUR TURN

List all the features of your shoe.

Ask a question at the start.

Use persuasive language.

Think of a good symbol.

Include a detailed picture.

Use some technical language.

Include a saying or slogan.

Design an advertising poster to 'sell' yourself. Make sure you include all of the features of an advertising poster. Share your poster with the grade, and discuss whether they do a good job of advertising you well.

Why are birds' beaks different?

Why are birds' beaks different?

Structure

A question in the heading

Introduction tells about topic

Series of facts telling how and why

Conclusion

Why are birds' beaks different?

Birds eat different things, so their beaks have different shapes for catching food and for eating it.

Birds of prey such as eagles have hooked beaks for tearing the flesh of animals they catch.

Waders (water birds) have long beaks for searching in mud for worms.

Kookaburras have stabbing beaks for catching snakes and other reptiles.

Nightjars have wide gapes (openings) for catching flying insects.

These birds would die if they had different beaks, because they would not be able to catch or eat their food.

Writer's Challenge   Types of beaks

List the four kinds of beaks found in the explanation:

1 _____   3 _____

2 _____   4 _____

Write an explanation

Birds' feathers

Use these facts to write an explanation about why birds have feathers.

Feathers keep birds warm.

Fluffy down feathers trap warm air next to skin.

They give wings and bodies a sleek, smooth shape.

Different colours and patterns identify birds.

Feathers help birds to fly.

Bright male feathers attract females.

Structure

A question in the heading

Introduction

Series of facts about feathers

Why do _____ **?**

_____

_____

_____

_____

_____

_____

_____

Conclusion

Work with your teacher to find out about a bird that cannot fly. Write an explanation for your grade about why the bird you chose cannot fly.

Why do birds sing?

Structure

Question in the heading

Introduction
Tells what the explanation is about

Series of facts
Tell how and why

Conclusion

Why do birds sing?

Many people think that birds sing because they are happy, but this is not true. There are two kinds of sounds birds make.

1 Song   Songs are used to:

attract a mate

warn other males

Stay out of my territory!

2 Call notes   Call notes are used to:

Honk, Honk! Keep together

Okay

Watch out!

I'm hungry FEED ME!

signal other birds   as a danger warning   baby birds call to their parents

Songs do not sound the same

The songs of the same kind of bird sound the same to us, BUT each bird's voice sounds different to other birds. Even in a crowded colony the parent birds can single out the voices of their own chicks.

Writer's Challenge   Match the bird to the sound it makes.

Bird sounds

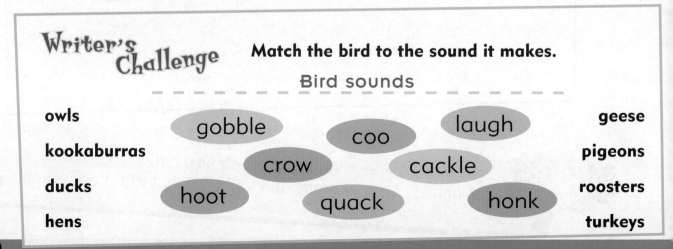

owls   gobble   laugh   geese

kookaburras   coo   pigeons

          crow   cackle

ducks   hoot   roosters

hens   quack   honk   turkeys

Write an explanation

How do cats show their feelings?

How do cats show their feelings?

Cats have many different ways of showing their feelings.

Now it is your turn

The heading and the introduction are given to help you start. Choose two of the feelings from the fact file below and write a series of facts. Then write a conclusion.

When cats are _____ they show their feelings by

picture
and label

When cats are _____ they show their feelings by

picture
and label

Fact file

Cat feelings

Playful   They leap, jump, skitter and chase. They will chase anything—leaves, bits of string, ants.

Angry   They hiss, growl, spit and scratch. Their hair stands on end and their tail switches.

Frightened   Hair stands on end, they crouch down, eyes dart everywhere, tail switching.

Happy (content)   They purr, sit quietly, smooch you, roll over to get their tummy tickled.

More to do

Why are cats called felines? Look up the word in a dictionary. Then make a list of as many felines as you can.

The magic horse

Structure

Language featur

Title

Orientation

Middle

End

The magic horse

One night I was playing, and a magic rocking horse came to my open window. It was very small.

When I picked it up, it grew as big as a real horse.

The magic horse could talk. She said, "Hop on. I can take you anywhere. I can take you to Disneyland, to the Moon or the North Pole. Where do you want to go?"

I said, "I want to stay here." And there I stayed.

Kate, Year 2

When?
Who?
Where?

Action words
e.g. 'picked',
'grew', 'talk'

Talking marks
" "

Writer's Challenge

Your turn to write

Write a different ending for the story.

Write a story

Story beginnings

It is important that stories have good beginnings.
The beginning is called the 'orientation'. The beginning tells:

- Who is in the story
- When it happened
- Where it happened

Write your own beginnings for these fairy tales.
Remember to say who? when? and where?

The Three Pigs

Once upon a time ...

Jack and the Beanstalk

The Three Bears

Write your own story. Remember, it must have a beginning (orientation), middle (complication) and end (resolution).

NARRATIVE

Albert the dinosaur

Structure

Title

Orientation

Middle

End

Albert the dinosaur

Albert was a big dinosaur. He had many scales on his body. He was a meat-eater with big sharp teeth that could crunch bones.

One day Albert crept up on another dinosaur, but it swung around and saw him. The mother whipped him and he fell in the water.

Albert's heavy weight pulled him down and he drowned. Over the years, mud layered over him.

For millions of years he lay there.

One day a scientist found him and took him to a museum. The museum gave him a name.

It was Albertosaurus.

Brent, Year 2

Past tense e.g. 'was', 'crep 'swung', 'whippe 'layered', 'fell' 'drowned'

Action verbs

Time words e.g. 'one day' 'over the year 'for millions o years'

Writer's Challenge   Read the story again and answer the questions.

1 **Was Albert small and smooth? Answer:**

No, he was _____ and _____.

2 **What did he eat, and what kind of teeth did he have?**

He was a _____-eater with _____

_____ teeth that could _____

_____.

3 **What made Albert fall in the water?** _____

_____

Write a story

Brent's story was about a BIG creature.

Write a story about a tiny creature—perhaps an ant, a snail, a beetle or butterfly.

Structure

Title

Orientation (beginning)

What did she or he look like?

Where did she or he live?

Middle

Write all the things that happened

End

Once there lived a   called

One morning

More to do

Write a different ending for your story. If the story ends happily, write a sad one. If it is sad, write a happy one.

The seed that grew

Structure

Orientation

The middle paragraphs

Conclusion
What happens?
How have things changed?

Language featu

Many different thir happen in th story.

Once upon a time a farmer planted a tiny seed. It was so small you could hardly see it.

It stayed in the ground for a l-o-n-g time. The rain rained, the sun shone and the wind blew, until one day a very small, bright green shoot popped out of the ground.

A month passed, then two months passed, and still the rain rained and the sun shone and the wind blew.

The green shoot grew into a plant. After three months the plant grew into a small tree. It grew higher and higher and higher, until at last it became the tallest tree in the forest.

Then one day a tiny seed dropped to the ground from a branch right at the top of the tree.

The rain rained and the sun shone and the wind blew and a tiny shoot popped out of the ground.

A new tree had begun to grow and it was right underneath the tallest tree in the forest.

Writer's Challenge

Narratives always have a beginning, a middle and an end.

Draw three pictures to show what happened at the beginning, the middle and the end of this story.

THE BEGINNING

THE MIDDLE

THE END

Write a narrative

The giant beanstalk

Write a story about a bean that grew and grew. It could be Jack's beanstalk or one of your own.

Structure

Orientation

The middle paragraphs

Write about the different things that happened.

The conclusion

Make it a good ending sentence.

Once upon a time

Write about 'the lion who lost his roar', 'a mouse in the house' or any story of your own.

NARRATIVE

The fox and the stork: a fable

Structure

Title

Orientation

Middle

Conclusion

Moral
Both are even now. Fox realises he was wrong.

The fox and the stork

One day a fox asked a stork to dinner. The fox was so mean that all they had to eat was some thin soup in a shallow dish.

The fox gobbled his up, but the poor stork couldn't eat any because of her long narrow bill. She tried again and again, but it was no use! She was still hungry.

"Didn't you like my lovely soup?" asked the fox. "You didn't eat much."

"I can't lap food up as you do," cried the stork.

Next week the stork invited the fox to dinner. She smiled as she gave him a long thin jar full of milk and honey. It had a wonderful smell.

The stork poked her long bill into the jar and quickly ate every bit of her meal, but the fox couldn't even get his tongue inside. All he could do was lick the outside of the jar—and he was starving!

"Well, now you've paid me back," said the fox. "You couldn't eat my dinner, and I couldn't eat yours. Fair's fair"

European fable

Language featu

Past tense
e.g. 'was',
'gobbled', 'trie
'cried', 'smiled
'poked', 'couldn
'paid'

Action verbs

Time words
e.g. 'one day
'next week"

Fables: short animal stories having a moral or point.

Foxes in European stories are often sly or mean.

Writer's Challenge

Wrong food

These have been given the wrong food. Draw better food in the square beside each picture.

bone		knife / fork	
fish food		chops and vegies	baby food
baby's bottle			
dog food		fish food	children's food

YOUR TURN

Write a story

Write a fable about two animals that play tricks on each other and learn a lesson.

Structure

Title

Orientation — Once there lived a

who wanted to play a game with

"Let's play ," she said.

Middle — Write all the things that happened

End

Draw one of your characters

More to do

Write about the GOOD fox inviting the stork to dinner and it is just perfect. The stork is so happy at the end.

POETRY

My dreams

My dreams

I dream about...
sunshine and birds,
rainbows and bees,
shadows and stars
—and I am happy.
I dream about ...
lost in the zoo,
kidnapped in space,
monsters at night
—and I am scared.

A poem says a lot in only a few words.

Some poems rhyme, but this one does not.

The verses are the same size. Each line is the same length. There is a pattern. They start and end in the same way.

Words used in poems should sound pleasant when read aloud— a bit like a song.

These poems (or verses) by boys in Year 2 are short. They rhyme and they show the many things we dream about.

I dream about cars and bees.
I dream about dogs and fleas.
Bill

I dream about cats and dogs and parrots.
I dream about goldfish and carrots.
Iain

Writer's Challenge   Try one of these short verses

I dream about

and _____

I dream about

and _____

I dream about

and _____

I dream about

and _____

Write a poem about dreams

Remember

- Follow the style of the poems on the other side.
- Think of all the different things you dream about. Make a list.
- Select words that sound good when you say them aloud.

Write list here

List of things you dream about

○ flying
○ school
○
○

Title _____

_____

I dream about...

_____ and _____

_____ and _____

_____ and _____

—and I am happy.

I dream about...

_____ and _____

_____ and _____

_____ and _____

—and I am _____

sad or scared or excited or ...

_____

Poet's name (YOU!)

Draw a peaceful dream. Use soft, calm colours. Draw a dreadful dream. Use angry, loud, clashing colours.

Beans, beans, beans

There are all kinds of poems …

they can be short or long; serious or funny; sad or happy, and some can be fun just to read aloud—like this one.

Beans beans beans ← Title

Baked beans

Butter beans

Big fat Lima beans

Long, thin string beans

Those are just a few

Green beans

Black beans ← Short line

Big fat kidney beans

Jumping beans, too

Pea beans

Pinto beans

Do not forget Shelley beans

Last of all, best of all,

I like jelly beans.

Anonymous ← Author

Writer's Challenge   Look in the poem to find:

1 A word that rhymes with 'Shelley' _____

2 A word that rhymes with 'few' _____

3 Four words that begin with 'b' _____   _____

_____   _____

4 Four words that describe beans _____

Write a poem
Dogs dogs dogs

Use the poem on beans as the model for your poem on dogs.
Some of the words have been provided. You fill in the spaces.

Dogs dogs dogs ← Title

Black dogs
Brown dogs

_____ dogs
(3 or 4 words)

_____ dogs
(3 or 4 words)

Those are just a few

_____ dogs

_____ dogs

_____ dogs
(3 or 4 words)

_____ too
(3 or 4 words)

_____
(2 words)

_____
(2 words)

Do not forget _____ (2 or 3 words)

Last of all _____ (2 or 3 words)

I like _____ (2 or 3 words)

Your name _____

Author

Write your own poem. It could be about dogs or
beans, or any subject you like.

It might rhyme or it might not—but make sure it has
rhythm and sounds good when you read it aloud.

POETRY

Autumn leaves

Structure

Language featur

Title

Verses

• _6 verses_

• _3 lines in each verse_

• _Last two words of each verse rhyme_

Autumn Leaves

1
Leaves in my sleeves
Leaves in my hair
Autumn is leaving leaves everywhere.

2
Leaves in my dress
Leaves in my shirt
Autumn is throwing leaves in the dirt.

3
Leaves when it rains
Leaves when it blows
Autumn leaves leaves wherever it goes.

4
Leaves in the air
Leaves on the ground
Autumn paints leaves with never a sound.

5
Leaves in my ears
Leaves in my eyes
Autumn gives trees a winter surprise.

6
Leaves in my sleeves
Leaves in my hair
Autumn is leaving leaves everywhere.

Virginia Ferguson and Peter Durkin

Authors

'Leaves' repeated

'Autumn' repeated

Rhyming words

Writer's Challenge

Sometimes poems contain rhymes, other times they do not. In Autumn Leaves there are many rhyming words. Look in the poem for the words which rhyme with:

1 dirt_____

2 ground_____

3 surprise_____

4 hair_____

5 goes_____

6 sleeves_____

Make a list

Write 10 words which rhyme with 'trees'. _____

_____

Write a poem

Autumn, summer, winter or spring

Write your own poem. It could be about autumn, summer, winter or spring. Or it could be on a topic of your own choice.

tructure

itle

eave a space etween verses

uthor

Write a 'four seasons' poem, working in groups of four. Each person chooses a season and writes a verse for that season. Present the poem on an A4 page and illustrate it. Each group presents its poem to the class, and then displays it.

Writer's word list

a	didn't	I'm	of	they
about	do	if	off	thing
after	dog	in	oh	think
again	don't	into	old	this
all	door	is	on	thought
also	down	it	one	three
always	eat	its	only	time
am	ever	just	or	to
an	every	know	other	told
and	father	leaves	our	too
another	finally	left	out	took
any	find	like	over	two
are	first	little	people	up
around	for	long	play	us
as	found	look	put	very
asked	friend	made	ran	wanted
at	friends	make	really	was
away	from	man	red	water
back	fun	many	right	we
be	get	me	room	well
because	go	money	said	went
bed	going	moon	saw	were
before	good	more	say	what
best	got	morning	school	when
boy	had	most	see	where
brother	has	mother	she	while
but	have	Mr	should	white
by	heard	much	so	who
called	help	mum	some	why
came	her	my	something	will
can	here	name	started	wish
car	him	never	take	with
children	his	new	tell	work
colour	home	next	that	world
could	house	nice	the	would
couldn't	how	night	them	year
Dad	I	no	then	years
day	I'd	not	there	you
did	I'll	now	these	your

What I think about my writing

Things I can do

Colour in the stars when you are able to do the things on the list.
When you have coloured in all the stars, you become a Star Student.

- I can write and talk about things that have happened.

- I can write a letter and a thank-you note.

- I can write reports and descriptions.

- I can write instructions.

- I can write arguments.

- I can write advertisements and posters.

- I can write about why things happen.

- I can write stories.

Congratulations!
You are now a Star Student

- I can write poetry.

Signed: _____

TEACHER'S COMMENTS:

Student's writing profile

INDICATORS	E	C	B	N
1 Recounts				
• Uses recounts to retell past experiences				
• Establishes the when, where and who of a recount				
• Includes recount events in sequence				
• Writes additional information about the more important events of a recount				
• Writes a conclusion				
• Maintains tense				
• Uses action verbs such as 'saw', 'did', 'went'				
• Uses adjectives and adverbs to add to meaning				
• Uses linking words such as 'next', 'then', 'later'				
• Writes complete sentences				
• Varies sentence lengths				
2 Transactions				
• Writes simple notes to friends				
• Attempts simple letters				
• Attempts simple invitations				
• Discusses the purpose of simple surveys and questionnaires				
3 Reports				
• Discusses and understands the purpose of written reports				
• Introduces the topic at the start				
• Attempts a classification or generalisation				
• Begins to organise topics into paragraphs				
• Describes specific features of the topic				
• Uses a simple concluding, summarising statement				
• Uses some technical language				
• Uses simple conjunctions				
• Uses linking verbs such as 'has', 'belongs to'				
• Uses timeless present tense				
4 Procedures				
• Discusses the purpose and form of written instructions				
• Uses a procedure framework: purpose, materials and method				
• Includes the necessary steps of the procedure in sequence				
• Illustrates procedure to support the text, e.g. using labels and diagrams				
• Maintains simple present tense				
• Uses linking time words such as 'first', 'after', 'next'				
• Starts directions with a verb, e.g. 'stir', 'mix'				
• Uses action verbs				

INDICATORS			CODE	
	E	C	B	NA
5 Persuasive texts				
• Discusses reasons for writing expositions				
• Writes an opening statement that states personal position taken				
• Expresses ideas subjectively, e.g. 'I feel… '				
• Includes arguments that support position without logical sequencing				
• Provides some supporting evidence				
• Provides a concluding statement that re-states position				
6 Explanations				
• Discusses some examples of where written explanations are used				
• Attempts to explain links between cause and effect, e.g. 'because… then… as'				
• Begins to use objective language to explain phenomena				
• Attempts use of passive tense, e.g. 'is caused by'				
• Uses simple present tense, e.g. 'grows', 'falls'				
• Uses some specific terms for subject				
7 Narratives				
• Discusses why stories are written				
• Writes a suitable title				
• Provides some details of setting				
• Includes the who, when and where of the story				
• Writes about stereotypes such as fairies or witches				
• Begins to include simple complications				
• Introduces characters with some attempt at description				
• Attempts a resolution of the story, e.g. 'I was just dreaming'				
• Writes conversation with an attempt to use direct speech, exclamations and question marks				
• Uses conjunctions, e.g. 'because', 'if'				
8 Writing strategies				
• Usually uses capital letters at the beginning of sentences				
• Usually uses full stops at the end of sentences				
• Draws on knowledge of sight words and high frequency words when writing a text				
• Draws on knowledge of common letter patterns and letter–sound correspondence when writing a text				
• Reads own writing aloud and makes some corrections to clarify meaning				
• Begins to edit, check and make simple corrections in own writing				
• Uses correct pencil grip and maintains correct body position				
• Forms most letters of the alphabet correctly and tries to write in straight lines from left to right				

Text Types for Primary Schools

FACTUAL TEXTS

	BOOK 1	BOOK 2	BOOK 3	BOOK 4	BOOK 5	BOOK 6
Recount	• What I did yesterday • I remember crying • I went on a picnic • I like hearing the crickets • My special place	• The big fish • The new playground • Dog in the fridge • I fell in the river	• A visit to the zoo • Stitches in my head • A school excursion: the bird-walk • The day our duck egg hatched	• Our mud fight • It still makes my blood boil … • The day we left Jack behind	• A day in my life • The slug • A brush with a shark • A newspaper report: Camel fiasco a laughing matter	• Why me? • Stuck in the middle again! • Talking about me — a personal recount • A newspaper report: TV zaps memory
Transaction	• A party invitation • A thank-you letter	• A birthday card • A letter from Virginia	• A letter to the Kids' Council	• A letter to Mr Posini	• Invitation to join a music club	• A letter of agreement
Report	• How lemonade is made • Wasps • The robin	• The shapes of leaves • From sheep to jumper • Butterflies • Chickens	• Sharks • Dinosaurs • Polar bears • Bread • Our axolotl	• Lions • Tyrannosaurus • Mummies • ASIMO the robot	• Praying Mantis • Jupiter • Muscles	• Insect-eating plants • The Internet • From egg to tadpole to toad
Procedure	• How to make orange jelly • How to make a leaf rubbing • How to make mud bricks • How to make a fruit salad	• How to grow trees on tiny islands • How to make a floating flower • How to make a green hairy head • How to play Scissors, Paper, Rock	• Making a pizza • How to make mud pies • How to make pepper jump	• Yeast power • Pirate's treasure map • Making a worm farm	• How to make a compost bin in a soft drink bottle • Maps and directions • The four torn edges	• How to make a shadow puppet • How to make worm fritters • How to have a bath
Persuasive	• "I like …" • A sunsmart poster	• What we need in the world • Ice creams • Kangashoos	• Homework! Yes or no? • Cats make good pets • Poster: Cracklin' burgers	• Spaghetti • Sun bars	• Letter to a magazine • Bush dance poster	• A national disgrace • The coach's address • I think I'll become a vegetarian • Writing an advertisement
Explanation	• How does a plant grow? • How do spiders spin webs?	• Why are birds' beaks different? • Why do birds sing?	• Why can you see your breath on a cold day? • Why do moths flutter around lamps? • What are fossils?	• How are rainbows formed? • Why do stars twinkle? • Why do we feel dizzy when we spin around?	• What causes earthquakes? • Where does food go? • What causes thunder and lightning?	• Why do leaves change colour in autumn? • What causes the doldrums? • What is a red giant?
Biography			• Alice Grant — circus star	• Alexander Selkirk — marooned sailor	• Bert Facey — a "fortunate" man	• Mary Kingsley — African adventurer

LITERARY TEXTS

	BOOK 1	BOOK 2	BOOK 3	BOOK 4	BOOK 5	BOOK 6
Narrative	• The lion and the mouse • The scared elf • Two stories • The poor woman's wish	• The magic horse • Albert the dinosaur • The seed that grew • The fox and the stork: a fable	• The ants and the grasshopper • Princess and Oink • The magic cloak: a folk tale from Norway	• A Norwegian myth • The sick camel • On the way to school • Prunella Pelican	• A Greek legend • The possum chase • The farmer and his sons	• Tourist eats crocodile • The starfish story • Around the bend
Information narrative			• Nan	• My shed • Holiday at Pickering's Hut	• My pop • Along the river track	• Where do writers get their ideas?
Poetry	• Jump or jiggle • Wishes • Quiet is …	• My dreams • Beans, beans, beans • Autumn leaves	• A poem about the senses • Things	• Word pictures • Over and under • Dirbs and gorfs	• He was … • Acrostics • What is … a million? • Fred and the mosquito	• Why? • Landscape • That was summer